LOOK WHAT REVIEWERS HAVE SAID ABOUT "VIDEO FAMILY PORTRAITS"

"An easily read and referenced book that reduces a complex undertaking to simple-to-follow steps."

★★★★ *The Philadelphia Inquirer*

"Provides extensive sample questions on a wide variety of subjects to help loosen up the camera shy."

★★★★ *The Washington Post*

"Serves a special purpose besides teaching you the essentials of good videos." ★★★★ *Chicago Tribune*

"Will enable the genealogist to become a top-notch movie director and producer." ★★★★ *Los Angeles Times*

"The technical videotaping information is great." ★★★★ *The Dallas Morning News*

"Filled with insightful tips." ★★★★ *Boston Globe*

"The most complete book on this subject. You have laid out a series of question topics that make it infallible."

★★★★ *KIFV, Los Angeles*

"If you follow their guide you'll end up with something the whole family will value."

★★★★ *WAMU, Washington, D.C.*

"Open this book and you open your family to treasured videos of joyous gatherings."

★★★★ *The Albany Sunday Herald*

ABOUT THIS BOOK

How to Create a Video Family History is not a manual about how to operate your video equipment. Forget about step-by-step instructions and technical details. If you own a camcorder, you will be able to do everything described in this book.

How to Create a Video Family History will not only help you document your family history, but it will also provide you with ideas to do something more with your camcorder and an incentive to do it more often.

How to Create a Video Family History is the fun and easy way to help you discover your family "treasures" and pass on your family history, stories and memories — all year long!

How to Create a
Video
Family
History

The Complete Guide to Interviewing and Taping
Your Family's Stories & Memories

Rob & Laura Huberman

COMTEQ
PUBLISHING
Margate, New Jersey

Copyright © 2003 by Rob & Laura Huberman

Published by:
    ComteQ Publishing
    A division of ComteQ Communications, LLC
    P.O. Box 3046
    Margate, New Jersey 08402
    609-487-9000 • Fax 609-822-4098
    Email: publisher@ComteQ.com
    Website: www.ComteQcom.com

ISBN 0-9674074-4-3
Library of Congress Control Number: 2002093383

Book and cover design: Rob Huberman
Photos: Rob Huberman

Printed in the United States of America
10 9 8 7 6 5 4 3 2 1

Dedicated to our parents — Abe & Rae and Jay & Juel

To our children — Joshua & Jason

and to all those who wanted to know, but didn't know what to ask.

Contents

3 INTERVIEWING BASICS

xii

Video Family History

Contents

6 100 QUESTIONS YOU'D NEVER THINK TO ASK

7 140 QUESTIONS FOR EVERY HOLIDAY

Contents

ABOUT THE AUTHORS

xvii
Video Family History

ACKNOWLEDGEMENTS

We'd like to acknowledge the following people for their encouragement and support of our current publishing efforts: Tom Parshall; Jack & Leslie Engelhard, Alan Sorkowitz & Michele Rappoport; Jan & Barry Weber; Leo & Ann Lieberman, Ellen & Gregg Lichtenstein, Sid & Evelyn Ascher, Dan Ojserkis; Marc Robinson; Jay Lappin and Chloe Chipkin.

We'd also like to acknowledge the following people for their encouragement and support of our original publishing and video efforts: Mitch & Brad Huberman, Jeffrey Janis, Leonard & Ida Mendelsohn, Dennis Dickerson, Diane Maple, and Bob Davies.

Chapter 1

INTRODUCTION TO
VIDEO TAPING FAMILY HISTORIES

1 INTRODUCTION TO VIDEO TAPING FAMILY HISTORIES

What is a *Video Family History?*

A *Video Family History* is a family "storybook" narrated by members of your family — parents and grandparents, brothers and sisters, aunts, uncles, cousins or even yourself.

A *Video Family History* is a family "documentary" about your family's heritage and experiences you produce with your camcorder featuring relatives who knew your ancestors and can recall the significant places and events that shaped their lives.

A *Video Family History* is a family "heirloom" that turns your TV into a family history time machine — enabling you to pass on your family history, stories and memories and share them with loved ones and future generations — time and time again.

Watch your family history come alive!

What a difference today's video technology offers in documenting the sights and sounds of our lives — especially when compared to those old home movies that left us wanting to know so much more about the people they showed gesturing and expressing their words and feelings — *in total silence!*

Maybe you're already a "pro" at videotaping your family events and vacations. Or maybe your camcorder just spends a lot of time in the closet since the novelty of recording everything in sight has worn off.

Well, what have you taped so far?

Babies are big. Weddings are a must. Vacations use up lots of tape. There's the kid's school plays and sports events. And how about those family gatherings! You know, where your relatives pile out of the car and parade in with you poking the camera in their faces. Or those scenes around the dinner table as everyone waves at the camera while attempting to chew food and smile at the same time.

Now you possess hours and hours of memories on video tape. Most likely you've shown your favorite parts a few times and even mailed out copies of the best scenes to share with family and friends. Then, having been (hopefully) labeled, your tapes are stored away on a shelf where they'll collect dust for who-knows-how-many years.

Now you can discover and capture family "treasures."

There's no better time than the present to start documenting your family history, stories and memories by taking the time to interview and videotape your parents, grandparents and other relatives. The information you uncover will one day be priceless.

Everyone has a story to tell about their life, and given the right opportunity, most like to talk about their experiences. Sharing these stories often stimulates long-forgotten memories, which can lead to many more wonderful stories about your family that might otherwise have been lost forever — had you not taken the time to capture and document them. During a *Video Family History* interview, individuals sometimes even forget they are being recorded and just "take a trip down memory lane."

You don't need complicated equipment.

Compiling your *Video Family History* doesn't require complicated equipment or technical procedures. All you need is your camcorder, video tape, tripod, and any TV. If you're a video novice, refer to the chapter on *Video Basics* that explains in user-friendly language all the techniques you'll need to know to produce outstanding video recordings as well as helpful hints and safety tips to make video taping as easy as possible.

Our *Video Family Interview Guide* makes interviews easy.

All you need are the right questions to encourage people to talk to you and help guide them through their thoughts and experiences. Then let your camcorder capture their mannerisms and expressions as your questions explore not only your family history, but your subject's personality, thoughts, emotions and spirit. Your video tapes will be filled with the wealth of experiences and richness of life these special people have to offer as you compile your *Video Family History.*

On page 41 you'll find our comprehensive *Video Family History Interview Guide.* The interview guide comprises twenty-six categories of general topics that include over five

hundred possible questions to explore family history as well as to help prepare both subjects and interviewers for their recording session. Just follow the guide's suggestions and your interview session will be organized, informative, and enjoyable.

Opportunities to record family history are all year long!

Documenting your family experiences isn't limited to doing a one-time *Video Family History* interview! Much of what will become family history for your children and grandchildren is happening right now! So take advantage of many opportunities throughout the year to add to your *Video Family History*, such *as* when relatives visit or at family holiday gatherings.

Just make it a habit wherever and whenever you pull out your camcorder, to take a moment to focus it directly on each of the family members that are present — young and old — and *ask some questions!* Personal questions. Topical questions. Thought-provoking questions. Fun questions. Unusual questions. Questions that will enable you and your family to remember something special about each of them. Future generations who watch these tapes will not only get to "meet" their relatives, but also get to

experience their personalities and mannerisms — just what was missing from those old silent home movies.

In addition to the *Video Family History Interview Guide,* we've compiled hundreds of "not necessarily your everyday questions" for all kinds of occasions that will enable you to keep adding to your family history. By taking advantage of the video and interview tips in this book, along with our *Video Family History Interview Guide* and our year-round questions, who knows what "family treasures" you'll discover throughout the years.

All you need to do is *start asking!*

Chapter 2

VIDEO BASICS

2 VIDEO BASICS

First of all — you don't need a video degree.

As we've already mentioned, if you own a camcorder, chances are you know how to operate it well enough to produce a *Video Family History*. But for those who are video novices or those who might like some suggestions for improving the overall quality of your recordings, the following information will help familiarize you with the "technical" side of video interviewing to help your interview look professional and last for years to come.

You can use any kind of video equipment.

Today's digital, VHS, or 8mm camcorders make the job of producing a *Video Family History* easier than ever. Features and functions among camcorders are nearly identical, so each is excellent for producing your *Video Family History*. The most important consideration is the maximum recording time of your tape. For the highest quality,

record at standard play (SP) – typically two hours for VHS and Hi 8, 30 minutes for VHS-C, and 1 hour for digital Hi 8.

Choose a high quality video tape.

Video tapes come in regular and premium grades. Premium grade tapes are well worth their slightly higher price because they provide superior picture quality and hold up better when played over time. You should also use a brand new tape rather than recording over a used one. Besides the benefits in quality, there is less chance you'll encounter recording problems that can arise from using worn or slightly damaged tapes.

How to compose a good looking TV picture.

Television viewers are accustomed to watching television shows that are produced with multiple cameras and several camera angles. Since your "TV show" will use a single camera and possibly only one subject, this results in what is referred to as a "talking head" shot. To help you properly compose a video picture and to provide variety for your viewers, here are basic camera angles and tips for your *Video Family History* interview.

head room

Make sure you leave some room at the top of the picture so that the subject's head is not cut off or right up against the top of the TV screen. The rule is to keep the subject's eyes approximately one third of the way down from the top of the screen.

nose room

When shooting the subject's profile, leave a little extra room in front of the face and in the direction the subject is looking.

hand motions

If your subject uses his or her hands to enhance their conversation, make sure you occasionally zoom out to a wider shot to catch those hand motions and gestures.

cover shot
Usually your widest shot (zoom all the way out), which gives the television viewer an overall look at the subject and the location of the taping.

medium shot
Shows subject from approximately the waist to just above the head. This is a good shot to use if your subject uses his or her hands when talking.

chest shot
Shows subject from the chest to just above the head. This is a good shot to use throughout most of the interview.

close up

Shows subject from the top of the shoulders to just above the top of the head. An excellent shot for capturing facial expressions and making television viewers feel more intimate with the subject.

extreme close up

Shows only the face of the subject. This shot may not always be very flattering to your subject. Use sparingly to accentuate extremely expressive or emotional moments.

over the shoulder shot

Includes part of the interviewer in the shot. Use this shot when long questions are being asked or when the subject and interviewer are interacting. Gives the TV viewer the feeling of being a part of the questioning.

Improving "hollow" sound quality.

The distance you shoot video from is rarely the best distance for recording quality audio because the further you place a microphone from your subject, the more "hollow" their voice will sound and the more background noise will be noticed. Since you don't want to put your camcorder too close to your subject's face, the microphone ends up several feet away from them.

Although the camcorder's built-in mike still produces an acceptable sound recording, use of an external mike will significantly improve the voice quality of your *Video Family History*. Your best choices are a hand-held mike, a lapel (clip-on) mike, or a shotgun (directional) mike. A hand-held mike is typically less expensive and can be placed on a coffee table or chair near your subject. A lapel mike is tiny and can be clipped onto the subject's shirt or dress. The shotgun mike mounts to the top of the camcorder. (Check your local video or consumer electronics store for microphone recommendations that work with your camcorder.)

Improving uneven lighting.

Today's camcorders can produce a surprisingly good picture with relatively little light. A bright, evenly lit room, however, is still best for producing your *Video Family History*. (Light sources producing uneven lighting may be large picture windows in the background, bright lamps in corners or next to subjects, and reflective surfaces such as glass picture frames on the walls.)

Even a room that is evenly lit, such as by overhead fluorescent lights, may still require additional light to improve the video picture quality. This is because overhead lighting does not evenly light a subject's face and casts shadows downward from the brow, nose and lips. A very low wattage mini-light that mounts to the top of a camcorder (or that is sometimes built in) can compensate for these shadows. Make sure, however, that your subject does not find the light annoying or distracting. In that case, you might add some standard room lamps or brighter bulbs to existing lamps. Overall, direct light is more complimentary to your subject than is overhead light.

Preventing accidental erasure of tapes

After you have successfully completed your *Video Family History*, you will want to make sure that your work does not accidentally get erased. All video tapes are manufactured with a pop-out or sliding ERASE TAB just for this purpose, located on the long side of tape's case. When you finish recording on your tape, gently pry out and remove the tab. Now, even if you inadvertently press RECORD instead of PLAY on your VCR, no recording will actually take place.

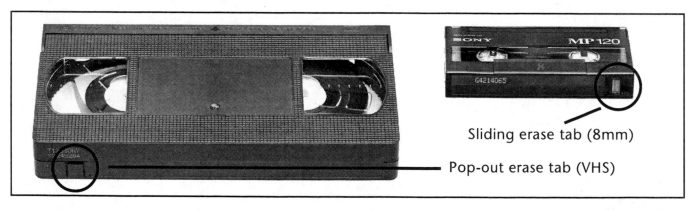

Sliding erase tab (8mm)

Pop-out erase tab (VHS)

Chapter 3

INTERVIEWING BASICS

3 INTERVIEWING BASICS

When is the right time to do a *Video Family History* interview?

There is really no best time to do your *Video Family History* interview. Whenever your subject is willing to be interviewed and you can get set up is the right time. It is, however, a good idea to make plans in advance that are convenient for both the subject and yourself. Keep in mind that family events and holiday gatherings provide great opportunities to record *Video Family History* interviews.

Where should I conduct the interview?

One of the most important considerations in conducting your *Video Family History* interview is a place that makes subjects as comfortable as possible. Try to seat them in a cozy chair or couch in a room with a relaxed setting, such as a living room or den. Avoid rooms with a cramped feeling like offices, kitchens, or closed-in bedrooms. Pick a

room that is not too noisy or distracting and tidy up unnecessary items or clutter before you begin the interview.

Do I need to prepare in advance?

Preparation before an interview is always important, especially if you wish to make the most of your interview time. By reviewing the *Family History Question Guide* along with the subject in advance, interviewers can become familiar with appropriate questions as well as have a chance to develop a rapport with the individual being interviewed. This review also enables subjects to anticipate upcoming questions, helps to "jog" their thoughts and memories, and generally improves their responses throughout the interview.

How should I approach elderly individuals about a video interview?

For some elderly individuals, the idea of doing a family history interview about one's life conjures up images of preparing a last will and testament. For this reason, great-grandparents or elderly family members may, at first, hesitate to be video taped. Assure

them that you are genuinely interested in learning about their lives and encourage them to preserve their stories on video. Even if they don't have the patience or stamina for an entire interview session, their *Video Family History* will become a family heirloom.

Can others be present during an interview?

Some individuals love to tell their stories to a large family group and won't mind who watches their interview. Others have a difficult time expressing themselves in front of people and tend to "clam up." In those cases, offer subjects the opportunity for privacy during their interview or limit the number of individuals present if it makes your subject feel more comfortable.

How much can I expect to record?

How much you'll be able to record will vary depending upon the subject's experiences, their willingness or ability to share them, and the amount of time available to do your interview. Therefore, before you embark upon your interview, you should inform individuals that they might not be able to share everything about their lives in a single

interview session. Consequently, express that you would welcome an opportunity for future interviews in which you can continue to learn more about them. Remember, taping *Video Family History* interviews are not necessarily one-time events. They can continue to be done for years to come!

Should subjects bring anything to the interview?

Old family photographs provide an excellent focal point for conversation about family history. They are also very useful for giving youngsters, as well as future generations, a glimpse of individuals being spoken about. Photos can be held up to the camera briefly while subjects point out individuals and explain their relationships. Your interview might also be enhanced by any personal items or momentos that subjects can talk about to help them share their story.

Is there any special advice for the interviewer?

Try to assume a relaxed posture throughout the interview. Sitting naturally should help to encourage your subject to do the same. Maintain eye contact with the subject, but

without seeming like you are staring. Present questions in a warm and expressive manner and try to avoid speaking in a monotone sounding voice that might discourage subjects from getting enthusiastic about their own responses.

Where should the interviewer sit?

A good position for the interviewer to sit is a little in front of the tripod with his or her back to the camera. Take care not to block the subject from the TV picture. The subject can then face both the interviewer and the camera when responding to questions. This position also allows you the option of including the interviewer on camera. (See "over the shoulder shot" on page 15.)

How do I get the interview started?

Double check to see if your subject requires anything before you settle in for your *Video Family History* interview. (It's thoughtful to have something available to drink nearby.) In preparation for the first question, try to get your subject a little loosened up. You can accomplish this by first engaging him or her in some "small talk." (A sample warm-up

conversation is included in the *Family History Question Guide* on page 45.) Once recording begins, the interviewer should state the date, the place where the interview is taking place, the name of the person being interviewed, and the subject's family relationship. Then move on to the first question.

Can I tape more than one individual at a time?

Sometimes married individuals feel more comfortable being interviewed as a couple and siblings enjoy sharing their memories as a group. Again, any opportunity to get individuals to share their personal story is a welcome opportunity to do a *Video Family History*. Just try to seat individuals comfortably and where you can conveniently record them as they interact. In these cases, your taping opportunity should take precedence over interviewing formality.

What if a subject's response needs clarification?

Sometimes one question is not enough to elicit all the information needed to cover a topic, or, your subject's first response does not provide you with enough details. This is

especially true when an individual responds with just a word or short phrase. Since this kind of response doesn't make for very interesting or informative conversation, as an interviewer, you need to be prepared to encourage that individual to tell you a little more.

Here are some questions you might ask to help them out:

What do you mean by that?

Could you tell me more about it?

Why was it that way?

Would you please elaborate?

What was that like?

How did that make you feel?

Can you give me more details?

Listen carefully to what is being said so that you can ask appropriate follow-up questions. After asking a question, wait a moment to give the subject plenty of time to formulate his or her response. Be certain that you do not pose your questions in a confrontational or demeaning manner. Also, refrain from expressing your own personal feelings or opinions in a way your subjects might interpret as contradicting them. Try not to interrupt unless the subject gets way off track.

What if the subject gets emotional or upset during taping?

Try to be sensitive to what is being said by your subjects during the interview. It's conceivable they might reveal extremely personal or disturbing thoughts which may not have been expressed for quite some time. If a particular story or memory causes the subject to become choked up or to cry, pause your recording for a few moments to allow them to regain their composure before moving on to the next question.

Can we take breaks during the interview?

If the subject becomes fatigued, it is a good idea to take a short break before attempting

to continue. Encourage the subject to get up and stretch, get something to drink, or go to the rest room until he or she feels comfortable enough to begin again. You are better off pausing as needed, rather than getting shortened responses because a subject has become fatigued during the interview.

How long should the interview last?

There is no set time frame for conducting your *Video Family History* interview. The endurance and willingness of your subject will most likely determine the length of the session. Plan, though, for a session to last about an hour to an hour and a half at most. Of course, if you are "on a roll," your session can last longer. Just have a second video tape ready, since one or two hours is the maximum length of most standard tapes at the highest-quality setting. If your subject is available, you might plan to do interviews in smaller sessions over a longer period of time and cover selected categories of questions in greater depth, rather than trying to rush through them all in one shot.

Is there a proper way to end the interview?

Keep in mind that it may be difficult to cover everything about an individual's entire personal history in a single taping session. Chances are that, after some time, subjects will feel that they have had enough for the time being, or you will sense that the session is beginning to drag. Call it quits and plan to shoot more at another time if your subject is willing. *Video Family History* interviews are not about quantity. Every minute you are able to record will become a treasure!

After completing the interview, thank your subject and let him or her know how much you enjoyed the opportunity to talk. Before you stop recording, offer subjects a chance to comment on the interview session or to express any final thoughts. You might even encourage them to give a special greeting to their current or future family members that will watch the tape.

One last tip about asking interview questions.

The questions in this book are organized in several ways to make them practical and easy to use. They are sometimes fun, sometimes serious, sometimes silly — just like

the experiences in real life! And while they do encompass many topics of conversation, holidays, and special events, they cannot cover everything. So please, make up your own questions or change these to your liking or needs.

Remember — you don't necessarily need long or elegant answers to every question for a worthwhile and enjoyable response. Use your judgement as to whether or not to probe for further information or just move on to the next question. Enjoy your interview and treasure the memories you are capturing!

As you compile your *Video Family History* over the years, attempt to include all your family members for as little or as much as they are willing to share. Over the years, each and every one of these conversations will contribute to your *Video Family History* and add to your collection of life's little treasures!

Chapter 4

JUST BEFORE YOU GET STARTED

4 JUST BEFORE YOU GET STARTED

Prepare your location.

The room you select will become the "set" for your *Video Family History*. Depending upon its layout or features, you might even consider rearranging some furniture, wall hangings, or plants to give your video picture added color and depth. Remember to remove unnecessary items that may clutter the look of your picture.

Make sure there's enough light.

Without enough light, your camcorder will provide a poor picture (flat colors, lack of detail, fuzzy images). A bright room, whether lighted by overhead lights, floor or table lamps, or windows, will provide a pleasant atmosphere and give your tapes a clear and vivid look. In dimly lit situations, additional lights may be necessary.

Prepare a comfortable spot for your subject to sit.

Select a location where your subject can sit comfortably throughout the duration of your taping session. If you will be displaying photos or memorabilia, make sure these items are accessible, yet out of the way when not needed. Leave enough room for other individuals to get in the picture if you plan to interview more than one subject at a time.

Avoid conflicting backgrounds and clothing.

Try to avoid very bright or very dark backgrounds. Dark backgrounds may force the subject to appear "washed out." Conversely, bright backgrounds affect picture quality by making the subject appear too dark. For this reason, don't use windows or other brightly lit areas as a background and keep bright lamps out of your picture. If possible, avoid very busy backgrounds (flowered wallpaper, bookcases, stereo equipment) since they can distract from your subject. Recommend that individuals wear bright or colorful clothing to help them stand out against the background in the TV picture.

Beware of sounds throughout the house.

Be aware of possible distracting sounds in the area where you are taping, such as telephones, home appliances, flushing toilets, street noise from open windows, and other individuals moving about the house. Take the phone off the hook, turn off stereos, dishwashers, clothes dryers, etc., close nearby windows, put the dog out, and try to limit general moving about in the area of your shoot. Remember, whatever your ears can hear will also be picked up on the tape!

Leave enough room for your video equipment.

Leave yourself enough space to set up your camcorder approximately five feet from your subject. This way, the equipment will not seem too imposing to subjects or cause them to become camera shy. Try to avoid making your area feel too cramped.

Be sure there's a plug nearby.

Make sure your location provides access to electrical outlets for any equipment you will be using. Have extension cords handy so that you have the freedom to set up your

equipment in the most convenient areas of the room. Use caution in laying cords across the floor in an area where someone might trip on them! Placing cords under a throw rug or taping them down with duct tape can help prevent possible accidents.

NOTE: Taping a *Video Family History* interview with just your battery power is not recommended because of the chances of losing power during the interview.

Chapter 5

**THE VIDEO FAMILY HISTORY
INTERVIEW GUIDE**

5 THE VIDEO FAMILY HISTORY INTERVIEW GUIDE

How to use the *Video Family History Interview Guide*.

The *Video Family History Interview Guide* is comprised of numerous questions and categories intended to help you organize a subject's personal history. The *Guide* provides a framework for subjects to organize their thoughts and stimulate their memories, while its friendly approach helps put them at ease as they begin to share their stories and experiences. Preselecting appropriate questions will help the interviewer to more smoothly conduct the interview.

For best results, the interviewer and subject should try to work together in advance of the taping, if possible, and decide which questions to ask during the interview. Those questions that pertain to the subject's experiences and background or those which prompt a special story or memory can be marked with an "x." (There are three sets of check boxes for interviews with different individuals.) In this manner, both the subject

and interviewer will know what to expect during questioning and be better prepared for a thoughtful and informative interview.

Keep in mind, these are only suggested questions. You are encouraged to alter questions or list additional ones that help your subject effectively tell his or her story. (Blank lines are provided throughout the interview categories as well as at the end of the *Guide* for your own questions.) Interview questions that seem too personal or do not pertain to a particular subject should be ignored.

You can also use the *Video Family History Interview Guide* as a work sheet on which to jot down notes or add follow-up questions during the interview. Try to keep note-taking to a minimum, however, since it can be distracting to the subject.

Since some questions are presented in a casual, conversational fashion, subjects may sometimes respond with a short or single-word answer. As a result, you may not feel that you've gotten an adequate response. In those cases, encourage subjects to clarify their responses or further elaborate. (See *What if a subject's response needs clarification?* on page 42.) Remember — *you do not have to ask every question.*

How to get your interview started.

Give your subject and interviewer about ten seconds notice before you begin recording, so that they may prepare themselves to speak. You should let the camera record a few seconds before you have the interviewer ask the first question. This gives the camcorder the necessary time to begin recording a completely smooth picture and makes sure that the first words spoken are not accidentally cut off.

It's a good idea to begin your *Video Family History* with a "cover shot" (see *Video Basics* page 30) to help establish the setting and familiarize the television viewer with the location of the recording. After the introductory remarks are complete, slowly zoom in to a "medium" or "chest shot" of your subject, which then helps the viewer to feel more a part of the interaction. In order to keep viewers interested throughout the interview, vary your camera shots from time to time, especially when lengthy answers are given.

Pay attention to what the subject is saying. You can then change your camera angles to enhance the dialogue and keep the viewer involved. For example, when subjects get excited or intense about a story, zoom in toward their face and hold a close-up shot.

When the conversation returns to normal, zoom back out to a different shot. Additionally, watch for the subject's use of hand expressions when making a point and similarly zoom out to a shot that includes these motions when they use them. Try to anticipate the subject's moves (such as bending over to pick up an object), so that you may react accordingly by changing your camera shot.

In this fashion you can avoid the "talking heads" image, which, after a while, can make viewers loose interest. Remember, continuous use of the same shot will make your tape monotonous and detract from your subject's answers.

Loosen up with a warm-up conversation and test recording.

In order to help your guest relax, engage him or her in a brief warm-up conversation (see sample below) while you make a test recording. [Press RECORD]

> *Hello. You are looking nice for your Video Family History interview. We are about to begin our interview and will cover the questions we discussed and selected beforehand. Are you comfortable? Can I get you anything?*

[Wait for a reply, then stop the test recording and rewind and replay the tape.]

> *Now we will playback the tape to make sure everything is working properly.*

[If the recording looks fine, then rewind to the beginning of the tape.]

> *Everything looks fine. If you are ready, then let's begin.*

[Press RECORD and begin your interview]

Let's INTRODUCE OUR SPECIAL GUEST

❏ ❏ ❏   What is your full name?

❏ ❏ ❏   What year were you born?

❏ ❏ ❏   Where were you born?

❏ ❏ ❏   How old are you now?

❏ ❏ ❏   Where do you currently live?

About Your FAMILY ROOTS (before coming to this country)

❏ ❏ ❏   What country(s) and city(s) did you or your ancestors come from prior to settling in this country?

❏ ❏ ❏   Can you name these individuals and tell us their relationships?

❏ ❏ ❏   What language(s) did they speak?

❏ ❏ ❏   What can you tell us about how these people lived?

❏ ❏ ❏   How did they earn their living?

❏ ❏ ❏   How large was their family?

❏ ❏ ❏   What was their family life like?

❏ ❏ ❏ What was their home like?
❏ ❏ ❏ What was their community like?
❏ ❏ ❏ What were the economic conditions in which they lived?
❏ ❏ ❏ What was the politics of their country?
❏ ❏ ❏ Did they have any special possessions?
❏ ❏ ❏ • customs?
❏ ❏ ❏ • skills?
❏ ❏ ❏ • problems?
❏ ❏ ❏ • interests?
❏ ❏ ❏ • hobbies?
❏ ❏ ❏ • pets?
❏ ❏ ❏ Can you describe any of their extended family, such as aunts, uncles, or cousins?

❏ ❏ ❏ _____

❏ ❏ ❏ _____

About Your FAMILY ROOTS (after coming to this country)

❑ ❑ ❑   Can you name the individuals who first made the journey to this country?

❑ ❑ ❑   What were their relationships to each other?

❑ ❑ ❑   What made them choose to come to this country?

❑ ❑ ❑   Was it difficult for them to leave?

❑ ❑ ❑   What did they bring with them?

❑ ❑ ❑   What did they leave behind?

❑ ❑ ❑   How did they get here?

❑ ❑ ❑   Do you know anything about what happened on their journey?

❑ ❑ ❑   Where did they arrive?

❑ ❑ ❑   Did their processing go smoothly?

❑ ❑ ❑   Were any other relatives or friends already here to greet them or help them get settled?

❑ ❑ ❑   Do you know in what year they settled and where?

❑ ❑ ❑   Can you tell us why they chose to settle there?

❑ ❑ ❑   How did their lives change after they arrived regarding:

❏ ❏ ❏   • economics?
❏ ❏ ❏   • socially?
❏ ❏ ❏   • politics?
❏ ❏ ❏   • religion?
❏ ❏ ❏   • occupation?
❏ ❏ ❏   • family/children?
❏ ❏ ❏   • language?
❏ ❏ ❏   • health?
❏ ❏ ❏   • recreation?
❏ ❏ ❏   • customs?
❏ ❏ ❏   • problems?
❏ ❏ ❏   How many generations of your family have lived in this country?
❏ ❏ ❏   Do you have any other special stories or recollections that you would like to share about your ancestors?

❏ ❏ ❏   _____

About Your FATHER

❑ ❑ ❑   What is (was) your father's full name?

❑ ❑ ❑   When was he born? Where?

❑ ❑ ❑   Where did he grow up?

❑ ❑ ❑   When did he die? Where?

❑ ❑ ❑   What did he die from?

❑ ❑ ❑   How old was he when he died?

❑ ❑ ❑   What do you know about his childhood?

❑ ❑ ❑   Did he have any siblings? What are (were) their names?

❑ ❑ ❑   What was his birth order?

❑ ❑ ❑   What did he look like? (height, weight, hair color, eyes, complexion, etc.)

❑ ❑ ❑   What can you tell us about his current or last occupation?

❑ ❑ ❑   Where and when did he pursue his occupation?

❑ ❑ ❑   Did he ever change occupations?

❑ ❑ ❑   What kind of a father was he?

❑ ❑ ❑   What kinds of things did he enjoy doing?

❏ ❏ ❏   Did he have any hobbies or special talents?

❏ ❏ ❏   What did you enjoy doing together as a child?

❏ ❏ ❏   • As a teen?

❏ ❏ ❏   • As an adult?

❏ ❏ ❏   Can you tell us about any of his special accomplishments or achievements?

❏ ❏ ❏   How did he influence you?

❏ ❏ ❏   What did you learn from him?

❏ ❏ ❏   Is there anything he could do that no one else could do?

❏ ❏ ❏   Did you have a special nickname for him? Did he for you?

❏ ❏ ❏   What were his strongest traits? Weakest?

❏ ❏ ❏   What do you most remember about him?

❏ ❏ ❏   Do you have any other special stories or recollections about your father that you would like to share?

❏ ❏ ❏   _____

About Your MOTHER

❑ ❑ ❑ What is (was) your mother's full name?
❑ ❑ ❑ When was she born? Where?
❑ ❑ ❑ Where did she grow up?
❑ ❑ ❑ When did she die? Where?
❑ ❑ ❑ What did she die from?
❑ ❑ ❑ How old was she when she died?
❑ ❑ ❑ What do you know about her childhood?
❑ ❑ ❑ Did she have any siblings? What are (were) their names?
❑ ❑ ❑ What was her birth order?
❑ ❑ ❑ What did she look like? (height, weight, hair color, eyes, complexion, etc.)
❑ ❑ ❑ What can you tell us about her current or last occupation?
❑ ❑ ❑ Where and when did she pursue her occupation?
❑ ❑ ❑ Did she ever change occupations?
❑ ❑ ❑ What kind of a mother was she?
❑ ❑ ❑ What kinds of things did she enjoy doing?

❏ ❏ ❏   Did she have any hobbies or special talents?

❏ ❏ ❏   What did you enjoy doing together as a child?

❏ ❏ ❏   • As a teen?

❏ ❏ ❏   • As an adult?

❏ ❏ ❏   Can you tell us about any of her special accomplishments or achievements?

❏ ❏ ❏   How did she influence you?

❏ ❏ ❏   What did you learn from her?

❏ ❏ ❏   Is there anything she could do that no one else could do?

❏ ❏ ❏   Did you have a special nickname for her? Did she for you?

❏ ❏ ❏   What were her strongest traits? Weakest?

❏ ❏ ❏   What do you most remember about her?

❏ ❏ ❏   Do you have any other special stories or recollections about your mother that you would like to share?

❏ ❏ ❏   _____

About Your PARENTS MARRIAGE & FAMILY LIFE

❏ ❏ ❏ Do you know how, where, and when your parents met?

❏ ❏ ❏ At what age were they married?

❏ ❏ ❏ Was it the first marriage for each?

❏ ❏ ❏ If not, what can you tell us about his or her previous one?

❏ ❏ ❏ What kind of wedding did they have?

❏ ❏ ❏ How old were they when they had their first child?

❏ ❏ ❏ How many children did they have?

❏ ❏ ❏ How would you describe their marriage?

❏ ❏ ❏ Were your parents more outgoing or private people?

❏ ❏ ❏ How did your parents influence you concerning:

❏ ❏ ❏ • religion?

❏ ❏ ❏ • money?

❏ ❏ ❏ • education?

❏ ❏ ❏ • social values/morals?

❏ ❏ ❏ • relating to other people?

❑ ❑ ❑ • children?
❑ ❑ ❑ • work?
❑ ❑ ❑ • politics?
❑ ❑ ❑ • marriage?
❑ ❑ ❑ • occupations?
❑ ❑ ❑ • family values?
❑ ❑ ❑ Did your parents
❑ ❑ ❑ • travel?
❑ ❑ ❑ • fight?
❑ ❑ ❑ • have parties?
❑ ❑ ❑ • share the same interests?
❑ ❑ ❑ • spend a lot of time together?
❑ ❑ ❑ • belong to any organizations?
❑ ❑ ❑ What were your parents' feelings regarding discipline?
❑ ❑ ❑ Would you describe your parents as protective?
❑ ❑ ❑ • What was this like for you?

❑ ❑ ❑ Did your parents have any health problems?

❑ ❑ ❑ What were some of your parents' hobbies or leisure activities?

❑ ❑ ❑ What can you tell us about some of your parents' special friends?

❑ ❑ ❑ What kinds of things made your parents happy? Sad?

❑ ❑ ❑ Do you have any special stories or recollections about your parents that you would like to share?

❑ ❑ ❑ _____

❑ ❑ ❑ _____

❑ ❑ ❑ _____

❑ ❑ ❑ _____

❑ ❑ ❑ _____

About Your SIBLINGS

❏ ❏ ❏ Do you have any brothers or sisters?
❏ ❏ ❏ What are their names and birth order?
❏ ❏ ❏ What are their age differences?
❏ ❏ ❏ When and where were your siblings born?
❏ ❏ ❏ Where are they now?
❏ ❏ ❏ Can you name or describe their family members?
❏ ❏ ❏ How did you get along with each of them growing up?
❏ ❏ ❏ How do you get along with each of them now?
❏ ❏ ❏ What do they do for a living?
❏ ❏ ❏ Do you have any other special stories or recollections about your siblings that you would like to share?

❏ ❏ ❏ _____

❏ ❏ ❏ _____

About Your CHILDHOOD

❑ ❑ ❑ Where did you grow up?

❑ ❑ ❑ What was it like where you grew up?

❑ ❑ ❑ Did you live there for a long time or did you move around a lot growing up?

❑ ❑ ❑   • How did you like that and how did it affect your childhood?

❑ ❑ ❑ Were you:

❑ ❑ ❑   • happy as a child?

❑ ❑ ❑   • more introverted or extroverted?

❑ ❑ ❑   • obedient or disobedient to your parents or to authority figures?

❑ ❑ ❑   • popular?

❑ ❑ ❑   • athletic?

❑ ❑ ❑   • over or under weight?

❑ ❑ ❑ What is your earliest memory?

❑ ❑ ❑ Who were some of your special friends?

❑ ❑ ❑ What can you tell us about your interests or activities?

❑ ❑ ❑ Tell us about any childhood achievements, accomplishments, or recognition.

❏ ❏ ❏ Who were your childhood role models or heroes?
❏ ❏ ❏ • How did you identify with them?
❏ ❏ ❏ Did you ever get into trouble?
❏ ❏ ❏ Did you ever run away from home? What happened?
❏ ❏ ❏ Did your parents punish you? How?
❏ ❏ ❏ Is there any childhood experience that dramatically changed your life?
❏ ❏ ❏ What was dating like when you were a young adult?
❏ ❏ ❏ Who is the first person you had a crush on?
❏ ❏ ❏ Who had a crush on you?
❏ ❏ ❏ When was the first time you fell in love?
❏ ❏ ❏ • Can you tell us about it?
❏ ❏ ❏ Did you ever have any health problems?
❏ ❏ ❏ What was your most memorable childhood experience?
❏ ❏ ❏ What was your most frustrating childhood experience?
❏ ❏ ❏ What was your most embarrassing childhood experience?
❏ ❏ ❏ What did you want to be when you grew up?

❏ ❏ ❏ Did you have any special travel experiences?
❏ ❏ ❏ What was your fondest possession?
❏ ❏ ❏ What did you always want that you never had?
❏ ❏ ❏ Who was the nicest person you ever knew? Meanest?
❏ ❏ ❏ Who was your best friend?
❏ ❏ ❏ Do you have any other special stories or recollections about your childhood that you would like to share?

❏ ❏ ❏ _____

❏ ❏ ❏ _____

❏ ❏ ❏ _____

❏ ❏ ❏ _____

❏ ❏ ❏ _____

About Your MARRIAGE

- When did you meet your spouse? How? Where?
- What were your first impressions of him/her?
- Did you think that he/she would be the "right" person?
- When did you know you had fallen in love?
- Where and when did you (your spouse) propose?
- How did you feel about getting married?
- How did your parents feel?
- What was your maiden name?
- When and where did you get married?
- What kind of wedding did you have and how many people attended?
- Who were the best man and maid of honor?
- Where did you spend your honeymoon?
- What do you remember about it?
- Do you have any special wedding memories?
- How long have (had) you been married?

❏ ❏ ❏ Had you been married before?

❏ ❏ ❏ What was the name of your previous spouse?

❏ ❏ ❏ What can you tell us about that marriage?

❏ ❏ ❏ Do you have any children from that previous marriage?

❏ ❏ ❏ When did your spouse pass away? Where? How did it happen?

❏ ❏ ❏ Did you remarry? To whom, where & when?

❏ ❏ ❏ Do you have any other special stories or recollections about your marriage that you would like to share?

❏ ❏ ❏ Do you have any advice you would like to share about marriage?

❏ ❏ ❏ _____

❏ ❏ ❏ _____

❏ ❏ ❏ _____

About Your BABIES

❏ ❏ ❏ Did you prepare for the birth of your first child? How?

❏ ❏ ❏ What were your pregnancies like?

❏ ❏ ❏ Were your babies planned or a surprise?

❏ ❏ ❏ Who are your babies named after?

❏ ❏ ❏ Can you share any special memories of your pregnancy and/or delivery?

❏ ❏ ❏ What did you think/feel when you first saw your baby?

❏ ❏ ❏ How did you prepare for your baby's arrival at home?

❏ ❏ ❏ Where did your baby sleep?

❏ ❏ ❏ What were the nightly feedings like for you and your spouse?

❏ ❏ ❏ How did your life change after the birth of you children?

❏ ❏ ❏   • What changed the most?

❏ ❏ ❏ Did you breast or bottle feed your children?

❏ ❏ ❏ What in particular do you remember about the first year of being a new parent?

❏ ❏ ❏ Do you have any other special stories or recollections about your babies that you would like to share?

About Your CHILDREN

❏ ❏ ❏ What are the full names of your children?

❏ ❏ ❏ When was each born? Where?

❏ ❏ ❏ What are their current ages?

❏ ❏ ❏ Were all of your children planned?

❏ ❏ ❏ Did you lose any children? What happened?

❏ ❏ ❏ Did you find raising your children to be a difficult or easy task?

❏ ❏ ❏ • What made it so?

❏ ❏ ❏ How did children affect and/or change your:

❏ ❏ ❏ • daily routine?

❏ ❏ ❏ • work?

❏ ❏ ❏ • relationship with your spouse?

❏ ❏ ❏ • relationship with your parents?

❏ ❏ ❏ • social life?

❏ ❏ ❏ • outlook on life?

❏ ❏ ❏ Did you have any help in raising your children?

❑ ❑ ❑ Did you take family trips with the children? Where and when?

❑ ❑ ❑ • Which were some of the most memorable?

❑ ❑ ❑ What were some of your most trying moments as a parent?

❑ ❑ ❑ What were some of your worst experiences in raising a child?

❑ ❑ ❑ What were some of the funniest experiences?

❑ ❑ ❑ What were some of the most rewarding experiences?

❑ ❑ ❑ How did you discipline your children?

❑ ❑ ❑ Did your children ever have any serious health problems?

❑ ❑ ❑ Who was most responsible for disciplining your children?

❑ ❑ ❑ What did you think your children would become when they grew up?

❑ ❑ ❑ Did your children spend much time with any particular relatives?

❑ ❑ ❑ What are your fondest memories regarding your children?

❑ ❑ ❑ What are some of the things that make you proud as a parent?

❑ ❑ ❑ Do you have any other special stories or recollections about your children that you would like to share?

❑ ❑ ❑ Are there any thoughts you would like your children to remember about themselves?

About Your Other RELATIVES

❑ ❑ ❑ Who are (were) your favorite relatives?

❑ ❑ ❑ Whom do (did) you most admire and why?

❑ ❑ ❑ Do you still live close to any relatives? Who?

❑ ❑ ❑ How often do you visit with your relatives?

❑ ❑ ❑ Do you have any special memories related to these visits?

❑ ❑ ❑ Did any relative particularly influence you? In what way?

❑ ❑ ❑ Do you have god-parents?

❑ ❑ ❑   • What are their names and what can you tell us about them?

❑ ❑ ❑ Would you like to share any memories about the loss of a relative?

❑ ❑ ❑ Did you ever enter into a business or other venture with a relative?

❑ ❑ ❑   • How did the business relationship affect your personal one?

❑ ❑ ❑ Do you have any other special stories or recollections about your relatives that you would like to share?

❑ ❑ ❑ _____

About Your IN-LAWS

❏ ❏ ❏   Who are your in-laws?

❏ ❏ ❏   How well were you accepted into your spouse's family?

❏ ❏ ❏   How well was your spouse accepted into your family?

❏ ❏ ❏   How do you get along with your in-laws now?

❏ ❏ ❏   • Has it always been that way?

❏ ❏ ❏   Do you have any other special stories or recollections about your in-laws that you would like to share?

❏ ❏ ❏   _____

❏ ❏ ❏   _____

❏ ❏ ❏   _____

❏ ❏ ❏   _____

About Being GRANDPARENTS

❏ ❏ ❏ When did you first become a grandparent?

❏ ❏ ❏ • How old were you at the time?

❏ ❏ ❏ • What did it feel like?

❏ ❏ ❏ How many grandchildren do you have?

❏ ❏ ❏ • What are their names?

❏ ❏ ❏ Did you help to raise your grandchildren?

❏ ❏ ❏ • What were the circumstances?

❏ ❏ ❏ What is the best thing about being a grandparent?

❏ ❏ ❏ How often do you get to see your grandchildren?

❏ ❏ ❏ What do you like to do with your grandchildren?

❏ ❏ ❏ Are you a great-grandparent?

❏ ❏ ❏ • How is that different from being a grandparent?

❏ ❏ ❏ What are your great grandchildren's names?

❏ ❏ ❏ Do you have any other special stories or recollections about your grandchildren that you would like to share?

❑ ❑ ❑ Do you have any special thoughts you would like your grandchildren to remember about themselves?

❑ ❑ ❑ _____

❑ ❑ ❑ _____

❑ ❑ ❑ _____

❑ ❑ ❑ _____

❑ ❑ ❑ _____

❑ ❑ ❑ _____

❑ ❑ ❑ _____

About Your EDUCATION

❑ ❑ ❑   What was the name and location of your:

❑ ❑ ❑   • nursery school?

❑ ❑ ❑   • grammar school?

❑ ❑ ❑   • junior & senior high?

❑ ❑ ❑   • college or university?

❑ ❑ ❑   • post-graduate school?

❑ ❑ ❑   • other schools? (vocational, special training)

❑ ❑ ❑   What was your grade school like?

❑ ❑ ❑   How did you get to school everyday?

❑ ❑ ❑   What were your favorite grade school subjects?

❑ ❑ ❑   What kind of student were you?

❑ ❑ ❑   Did your parents help you with your school work?

❑ ❑ ❑   Were getting good grades important to you?

❑ ❑ ❑   • What happened if you didn't get good marks?

❑ ❑ ❑   Did you have any particularly influential or favorite teachers?

❏ ❏ ❏ Who were your best school friends?

❏ ❏ ❏ What are some of your best school memories?

❏ ❏ ❏ Did you ever "play hooky" from school?

❏ ❏ ❏   • What did you do instead of going to school?

❏ ❏ ❏   • Did you ever get caught? What happened?

❏ ❏ ❏ What were some of your worst educational experiences?

❏ ❏ ❏ What was your high school like?

❏ ❏ ❏ How well did you do in high school?

❏ ❏ ❏ What were your extra-curricular activities? (clubs, sports, jobs, etc.)

❏ ❏ ❏ Did you have any accomplishments or special recognition?

❏ ❏ ❏ Did you ever know anyone who dropped out of school?

❏ ❏ ❏ What was your college like?

❏ ❏ ❏ How big a school was it?

❏ ❏ ❏ What did you major in? Minor?

❏ ❏ ❏ Did you receive any scholarships?

❏ ❏ ❏ Where did you live during college?

❏ ❏ ❏ Did you have to work your way through college?

❏ ❏ ❏ What kind of job did you have?

❏ ❏ ❏ What was life like on campus?

❏ ❏ ❏ Did you belong to a fraternity or sorority?

❏ ❏ ❏ How has your college degree helped your career?

❏ ❏ ❏ Do you have any thoughts about education that you would like to pass on to your children or grandchildren?

❏ ❏ ❏ Do you have any other special stories or recollections about your education that you would like to share?

❏ ❏ ❏ _____

❏ ❏ ❏ _____

❏ ❏ ❏ _____

About HOMES and WHERE YOU'VE LIVED

❑ ❑ ❑ Can you list chronologically the places where you resided and when?

❑ ❑ ❑ What was your favorite residence and its location?

❑ ❑ ❑ Are there any special circumstances relating to a place you lived?

❑ ❑ ❑ Do you have any special memories connected with a particular home?

❑ ❑ ❑ When did you move out of your parent's house?

❑ ❑ ❑ Did you live by yourself or have roommates?

❑ ❑ ❑ Did any other family members ever live with you?

❑ ❑ ❑ What do you remember about any of your neighbors?

❑ ❑ ❑ Do you have any other special stories or recollections about your homes or where you've lived that you would like to share?

❑ ❑ ❑ _____

❑ ❑ ❑ _____

About Your EMPLOYMENT HISTORY

❑ ❑ ❑ What was your first job and how did you get it?

❑ ❑ ❑ • How old were you?

❑ ❑ ❑ What were your responsibilities? Did you like it?

❑ ❑ ❑ What do you do now?

❑ ❑ ❑ How long have you been doing it?

❑ ❑ ❑ What were you doing when you retired?

❑ ❑ ❑ • How old were you?

❑ ❑ ❑ Was there anyone who particularly influenced your career choice?

❑ ❑ ❑ Can you describe chronologically other jobs that you have had?

❑ ❑ ❑ Were you ever unemployed for a period of time?

❑ ❑ ❑ • What were the circumstances?

❑ ❑ ❑ • How did that affect your life?

❑ ❑ ❑ Was any job particularly influential in bringing about change in your life?

❑ ❑ ❑ • In what way?

❑ ❑ ❑ What are some of your fondest job memories?

❏ ❏ ❏ What were some of your most frustrating job related experiences?
❏ ❏ ❏ What was the best job you ever had and why?
❏ ❏ ❏ What was the worst job you ever had and why?
❏ ❏ ❏ Do you have any other special stories or recollections about your employment that you would like to share?

❏ ❏ ❏ _____

❏ ❏ ❏ _____

❏ ❏ ❏ _____

❏ ❏ ❏ _____

❏ ❏ ❏ _____

About Your FRIENDS

❑ ❑ ❑   Who are (were) your closest friends?

❑ ❑ ❑   Where, when and how did you meet?

❑ ❑ ❑   Can you tell us about the last time you saw them?

❑ ❑ ❑   How often do you see your best friends? Where do they live now?

❑ ❑ ❑   What kinds of things do (did) you like to do together?

❑ ❑ ❑   What do (did) you like or admire most about your closest friend?

❑ ❑ ❑   What was the nicest thing a friend ever did for you?

❑ ❑ ❑   What was the nicest thing you ever did for a friend?

❑ ❑ ❑   Did you ever end a friendship over a disagreement or misunderstanding?

❑ ❑ ❑   What is the most important thing you have learned from a friend?

❑ ❑ ❑   Do you have any other special stories or recollections about your friends that you would like to share?

❑ ❑ ❑   _____

About Your HEALTH

❏ ❏ ❏ Do you have a secret to keeping healthy?
❏ ❏ ❏ Did you ever have a serious health problem?
❏ ❏ ❏ • Can you tell us how and when it started? How long did it last?
❏ ❏ ❏ • How did it affect you?
❏ ❏ ❏ Do you have any regular exercise routine?
❏ ❏ ❏ Did you ever have a physical disability? How and when did it occur?
❏ ❏ ❏ •What impact did it have on your life?
❏ ❏ ❏ Do you have any conditions for which you regularly take medicine?
❏ ❏ ❏ Did you ever have a close call with death?
❏ ❏ ❏ • Do you wish to share any thoughts about the circumstances?
❏ ❏ ❏ Do you have any other special stories or recollections about your health that you would like to share?

❏ ❏ ❏ _____

About Your RELIGIOUS BELIEFS

❑ ❑ ❑ What is your religion?

❑ ❑ ❑ • Were you raised this way?

❑ ❑ ❑ • If not, with what religion were you raised and why did you change?

❑ ❑ ❑ What role has religion played in your life?

❑ ❑ ❑ Were your parents actively religious?

❑ ❑ ❑ What did your parents teach you about religion?

❑ ❑ ❑ What formal religious schooling did you have?

❑ ❑ ❑ Did you take an active role in your place of worship?

❑ ❑ ❑ What were your favorite religious holidays and why?

❑ ❑ ❑ What kind of religious activities does your family participate in?

❑ ❑ ❑ Has anyone particularly influenced your religious beliefs? How?

❑ ❑ ❑ Have you had any special religious experiences you would like to share?

❑ ❑ ❑ Have you ever experienced any religious prejudice?

❑ ❑ ❑ Can you tell us about it and when and where it occurred?

❑ ❑ ❑ • How did that affect you?

❏ ❏ ❏ Do you think religious practices have changed since you were a child? How?

❏ ❏ ❏ Is it important for your children and grandchildren to be religiously active?

❏ ❏ ❏ What religious message would you give to your future generations?

❏ ❏ ❏ Do you have any other special stories or recollections about your religious beliefs that you would like to share?

❏ ❏ ❏ _____

❏ ❏ ❏ _____

❏ ❏ ❏ _____

❏ ❏ ❏ _____

❏ ❏ ❏ _____

About Your RECREATION and LEISURE ACTIVITIES

❑ ❑ ❑ What do you most like to do for fun?

❑ ❑ ❑   • Have you always liked to do this?

❑ ❑ ❑ How do you like to relax?

❑ ❑ ❑ What are your favorite hobbies?

❑ ❑ ❑ What sports do (did) you play? When?

❑ ❑ ❑ With whom do you spend most of your spare time?

❑ ❑ ❑ What is your favorite TV show?

❑ ❑ ❑ What kinds of movies do you enjoy seeing?

❑ ❑ ❑ What kinds of books do you enjoy reading?

❑ ❑ ❑ Do you have any other special stories or recollections about your leisure activities that you would like to share?

❑ ❑ ❑ _____

❑ ❑ ❑ _____

About Your SPECIAL FAMILY OCCASIONS

❏ ❏ ❏   What are some of your favorite family occasions?

❏ ❏ ❏   What was something funny that happened at a family occasion?

❏ ❏ ❏   What was the most difficult family occasion you ever attended?

❏ ❏ ❏   What was the worst family occasion you ever attended?

❏ ❏ ❏   When was the last time you had a large family gathering?

❏ ❏ ❏   • Do you recall anything special about it?

❏ ❏ ❏   What is the next family occasion you look forward to?

❏ ❏ ❏   Do you have any other special stories or recollections about your special family occasions that you would like to share?

❏ ❏ ❏   _____

❏ ❏ ❏   _____

❏ ❏ ❏   _____

About Your MILITARY EXPERIENCES

❏ ❏ ❏ How many years did you spend in military service? Which years?

❏ ❏ ❏ Were you drafted or did you enlist?

❏ ❏ ❏ If you enlisted, what made you decide to do so?

❏ ❏ ❏ In which branch of the service did you serve?

❏ ❏ ❏ Where were you stationed?

❏ ❏ ❏ What was you highest rank?

❏ ❏ ❏ How did you earn your promotion?

❏ ❏ ❏ Did you serve in any wars? Which ones?

❏ ❏ ❏ Did you see any combat action? Where and when?

❏ ❏ ❏ • What can you tell us about those experiences?

❏ ❏ ❏ How did the war affect your:

❏ ❏ ❏ • business?

❏ ❏ ❏ • family & home life?

❏ ❏ ❏ • residence?

❏ ❏ ❏ • outlook on life?

❏ ❏ ❏   What do you remember most about the threat of war?
❏ ❏ ❏   What was the political climate of your community like prior to the war?
❏ ❏ ❏   • Did it change afterwards?
❏ ❏ ❏   Did you have any relatives who were killed in a war?
❏ ❏ ❏   • How did you and your family deal with that tragedy?
❏ ❏ ❏   Did you have any friends who were killed in a war?
❏ ❏ ❏   • How did that affect you?
❏ ❏ ❏   Did you have any close calls with death during the war?
❏ ❏ ❏   What are some of your most memorable military experiences?
❏ ❏ ❏   Do you have any other special stories or recollections about your military experiences that you would like to share?

❏ ❏ ❏   _____

❏ ❏ ❏   _____

A Little About YOURSELF

❏ ❏ ❏ What makes you happy?

❏ ❏ ❏ What really annoys you?

❏ ❏ ❏ What concerns you most right now about:

❏ ❏ ❏   • yourself?

❏ ❏ ❏   • your family?

❏ ❏ ❏   • your country?

❏ ❏ ❏   • the world in which we live?

❏ ❏ ❏ Have you ever rebelled against something or someone?

❏ ❏ ❏ What is one of your strengths?

❏ ❏ ❏ What is one of your weaknesses?

❏ ❏ ❏ What are you most proud of?

❏ ❏ ❏ What are you most ashamed of?

❏ ❏ ❏ Who are you named for?

❏ ❏ ❏ What did you want to be when you were growing up?

❏ ❏ ❏ How have you changed throughout the years?

❑ ❑ ❑   If you could go back and change anything, what would it be?
❑ ❑ ❑   Do you have a favorite joke or story you would like to tell?
❑ ❑ ❑   Do you have any other special stories or recollections about yourself that you would like to share?

❑ ❑ ❑   _____

❑ ❑ ❑   _____

❑ ❑ ❑   _____

❑ ❑ ❑   _____

❑ ❑ ❑   _____

❑ ❑ ❑   _____

About Your PERSONAL ACCOMPLISHMENTS or SPECIAL RECOGNITION

❏ ❏ ❏ What was the most prestigious public recognition that you have received?

❏ ❏ ❏ • How old were you at the time?

❏ ❏ ❏ • Who gave you this recognition?

❏ ❏ ❏ • Were any of your family members present?

❏ ❏ ❏ What is your fondest memory of a personal or non-public recognition?

❏ ❏ ❏ • Who gave you this recognition?

❏ ❏ ❏ • Where did it take place?

❏ ❏ ❏ • How old were you?

❏ ❏ ❏ Did you ever do something for which you think you deserved special recognition, but did not receive it?

❏ ❏ ❏ • How did you feel at the time?

❏ ❏ ❏ • How do you feel now about it?

❏ ❏ ❏ What would you say is your greatest or most satisfying personal accomplishment?

❏ ❏ ❏ Is there anything special on which you are currently working?

❏ ❏ ❏ What would you still like to accomplish?

❏ ❏ ❏ Do you have any other special stories or recollections about your personal accomplishments that you would like to share?

❏ ❏ ❏ _____

❏ ❏ ❏ _____

❏ ❏ ❏ _____

❏ ❏ ❏ _____

❏ ❏ ❏ _____

❏ ❏ ❏ _____

❏ ❏ ❏ _____

About The People, Places and/or Events that have had a SPECIAL INFLUENCE on Your Life

❏ ❏ ❏   What person has had the most influence on you?

❏ ❏ ❏   • In what way have they influenced you?

❏ ❏ ❏   • Have you ever let them know how much they influenced you?

❏ ❏ ❏   Was there any event during your childhood that had a special influence on your adult life?

❏ ❏ ❏   • school related?

❏ ❏ ❏   • friend related?

❏ ❏ ❏   • parent related?

❏ ❏ ❏   • discipline related?

❏ ❏ ❏   • vacation related?

❏ ❏ ❏   • other?

❏ ❏ ❏   What particular place has had an important influence on you?

❏ ❏ ❏   • Can you describe it?

❏ ❏ ❏   • What makes that place special?

❑ ❑ ❑   • At what time in your life were you influenced by it?

❑ ❑ ❑   • Do you still visit it?

❑ ❑ ❑   Did any historical or political event have a special influence on you?

❑ ❑ ❑   • When did the event occur?

❑ ❑ ❑   • Where were you at the time?

❑ ❑ ❑   Have you been particularly influenced by any new inventions, space exploration, medical discoveries or breakthroughs in scientific research?

❑ ❑ ❑   • Can you describe them?

❑ ❑ ❑   • How did they change your life?

❑ ❑ ❑   Have you ever experienced any natural disasters such as earthquakes, hurricanes, fires, etc. that had an impact on your life?

❑ ❑ ❑   What do you remember about the:

❑ ❑ ❑   • Great Depression?

❑ ❑ ❑   • 1st World War?

❑ ❑ ❑   • 2nd World War?

❑ ❑ ❑   • Korean War?

❑ ❑ ❑   • Viet Nam War?

❑ ❑ ❑   • first time you rode in a boat or train?

❑ ❑ ❑   • first time you drove a car?

❑ ❑ ❑   • first time you flew in an airplane?

❑ ❑ ❑   • first time you saw TV?

❑ ❑ ❑   • assassination of, or attempts to assassinate world leaders?

❑ ❑ ❑   • first man on the moon?

❑ ❑ ❑ How has the world changed since the events 0f 9/11?

❑ ❑ ❑ What was the most important event during your lifetime and why?

❑ ❑ ❑   _____

❑ ❑ ❑   _____

❑ ❑ ❑   _____

Do You Have Any SPECIAL MESSAGE or PERSONAL PHILOSOPHY That You Would Like To Share with Your Future Generations?

❏ ❏ ❏ Is there anything else you would like to say that you forgot to mention earlier?

❏ ❏ ❏ Are there any particular hopes or wishes that you have for your family that you would like to mention?

❏ ❏ ❏ Is there a motto by which you have tried to live your life?

❏ ❏ ❏ What do you think is the key to happiness?

❏ ❏ ❏ When you think of the future, what do you see?

❏ ❏ ❏ What closing message would you like to give?

❏ ❏ ❏ _____

❏ ❏ ❏ _____

❏ ❏ ❏ _____

ADD SOME OF YOUR OWN QUESTIONS!

❑ ❑ ❑ _____

❑ ❑ ❑ _____

❑ ❑ ❑ _____

❑ ❑ ❑ _____

❑ ❑ ❑ _____

❑ ❑ ❑ _____

❑ ❑ ❑ _____

❏ ❏ ❏ _____

❏ ❏ ❏ _____

❏ ❏ ❏ _____

❏ ❏ ❏ _____

❏ ❏ ❏ _____

❏ ❏ ❏ _____

❏ ❏ ❏ _____

❏ ❏ ❏ _____

Chapter 6

100 QUESTIONS YOU'D NEVER THINK TO ASK!

Can you...

keep a secret?
make a good cup of coffee?
parallel park in one try?
roll your tongue?
say your name backwards?
tell the difference between Coke and Pepsi?

Video Family History

 **Did you ever...**

bid at an auction?
break any bones?
dream you could fly?
drive cross country?
fall asleep at a movie?
find something valuable?
fly a plane?
forget your anniversary?
get food poisoning?
go swimming naked?
hold a snake?
lock yourself out of your house or car?

 # *Did you ever...*

meet a movie star?
save some one's life?
see a UFO?
sleep on a train?
smash something in anger?
lose something that belonged to someone else?
wake up in a place and not remember how you got there?
win a lottery?
get robbed?
get in a car accident?

 *Have you ever been ...*

arrested?
asked to leave?
bitten by a dog?
broke?
camping in the wild?
caught cheating?
embarrassed about your appearance?
hypnotized?
in a cave?
in a fist-fight?
in a limousine?

 *Have you ever been ...*

in jail?
in therapy?
mugged?
on a jury?
on a television show?
operated on?
ripped off?
thrown off a horse?
to a fortune teller?
told you look like someone famous?
too sunburned to put your clothes on?

 **Are you...**

allergic to anything?
a vegetarian?
charitable?
funny?
lucky?
optimistic about the future?
organized?
religious?
superstitious?
under a lot of pressure?
unemployed?

Do you...

believe in life on other planets?
file your taxes on time?
gamble?
have a custom license plate?
have a tattoo?
like surprises?
remember the Alamo?
sing in the shower?
smoke?
speak a foreign language?
stay in touch with old friends?
wear dentures or contacts?

 **Where were you when...**

the stock market crashed?
Pearl Harbor was bombed?
WWII ended?
Kennedy was assassinated?
a man first walked on the moon?
the 9/11 terrorist attacks occurred?
your first child was born?

 **What is your ...**

favorite joke?
favorite way to relax?
most frightening experience?
most precious possession?
favorite book?
favorite thing to eat?
favorite place to vacation?
favorite charity?
favorite vice?
favorite drink?
favorite imaginary place?
favorite TV show or movie?

 **What is the...**

best party you've ever been to?
biggest thing you've ever seen?
hottest (coldest) you've ever been?
longest you have ever gone without eating?
vegetable you hated most as kid?
most valuable thing you own?
fastest you've ever driven a car?
biggest mistake you ever made?
nicest thing you have ever done?
one thing you have always wanted to do?
secret to a long life?

Chapter 7

140 QUESTIONS FOR EVERY HOLIDAY

JAN · **New Years Eve**

How do you like to celebrate New Year's Eve?
What was the best thing that happened to you last year?
What was your New Year's resolution last year?
How well did you do in keeping it?
What is your resolution for the new year?

Martin Luthor King Day   JAN

What do you think is Rev. King's most important contribution to our nation?
How do you think things would be different if he had lived?
What African-American leader do you currently most admire and why?
How should this day be celebrated?

 FEB

Groundhog Day

Do you believe that if the groundhog sees its shadow
there will be six more weeks of winter?

Have you ever actually ever seen a groundhog?

What would you do if you woke up and discovered a groundhog on your porch?

Do you know the name of the most famous groundhog?

Valentine's Day FEB

Do you usually send or receive more Valentine's cards?
Whom do you send them to or receive them from?
Who was the first boy (girl) you ever kissed?
Who was your first sweetheart?

 FEB

Presidents Day

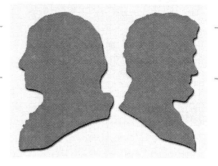

Who is (was) your favorite President?
Who would you like to see run for President?
Who was the greatest (worst) President ever?
What do you think of our current President?
What should our current President be doing differently?

St. Patrick's Day MAR

How do you like to celebrate St. Patrick's Day?
Do you know who St. Patrick was?
What would be a good dish to serve on this day?
Have you ever gotten drunk on green beer?

MAR   *Spring Begins*

What are you plans now that it's Spring?
Do you do Spring cleaning?
Do you plan to plant a garden?
What do you enjoy most about this time of year?

April Fools Day   ΛPR

What is the best April Fools Day prank you have ever played on someone?
What is the best April Fools Day prank ever played on you?
What is the most foolish thing you've ever done?
Do you easily fall for tricks played on you?

APR *Passover*

What do you know about the origin of this holiday?
Who leads your Seder?
What is the significance of this holiday to you?
Where do you hold your Seder?
Do you celebrate for two nights?
How do you feel about eating matzah for eight days?
Can you recite the Four Questions? In Hebrew or in English?

117

Video Family History

Easter   APR

What does this holiday mean to you?
Where do you celebrate this holiday?
Does your family do anything special in observance?
What was you favorite Easter egg hunt?
What is you favorite childhood Easter memory?
Who do you spend this holiday with?
Did you ever get a real bunny for Easter?

APR **Earth Day**

What is the biggest problem plaguing the Earth today?
What should be done to save the Earth?
Who is responsible for protecting the environment?
What are you doing to further this cause?

Cinco de Mayo   MAY

What do you know about the history of this holiday?
Who was the greatest Mexican hero?
What do you do to celebrate this holiday?

MAY   *Mother's Day*

What is the best advice your mother ever gave you?

What do you do for your mother on this day?

What is the nicest thing your children ever did for you on this day?

Armed Forces Day   MAY

Have you ever served in the Armed Forces?

Which is the most important branch of the military?

Should the U.S. have a national military parade?

Does the U.S have a strong enough military presence in the world?

Does the U.S. spend too much money on defense?

MAY   *Memorial Day*

Do you know anyone who was killed in action?
Do you fly the American flag on this day?
Have you ever visited Arlington National Cemetery?
What are your thoughts about those who have fought
for and died for our country?

Flag Day   JUN

Do you own an American Flag?
Do you fly it on holidays?
Where do you fly your flag?
Do you think it should be illegal to burn the flag?
What does the American flag symbolize to you?

124
Video Family History

JUN   *Father's Day*

What is the most important thing your father taught you?
What is you proudest moment as a father?
What have you learned about life as a father?
Do you have a favorite story about your father?

Summer Begins   JUN

What are your plans this summer?
If you could vacation anywhere this summer, where would it be?
What do you like to barbecue?
What was your most interesting summer job?

JUL   *Independence Day*

How do you celebrate on July 4th?

What does freedom mean to you?

What is the best fireworks display you have ever seen?

Did you ever play with firecrackers as a youth?

Labor Day

SEP

What do you most enjoy about your work?

What do you wish you had more time to do around the house?

What do you wish you could have been if you could be anything you wanted?

SEP **Back To School**

Did you look forward to going back to school?

Did you ever dream that you walked into class and they were giving a test you were not prepared for?

What school supplies did you used to get?

Who was you best (worst) teacher?

Autumn Begins   SEP

What do most enjoy about the change in seasons?
Did you ever go out into the country to see the leaves change color?
Do you have to rake a lot of leaves around your house?

 OCT *Columbus Day*

What do you think has been the most important
discovery during your lifetime?
What do you think has been the most important discovery to humanity?
Have you ever taken a cruise across the ocean?

Halloween OCT

What do you like to dress up as?

Did you ever get sick from eating too much candy after trick-or-treating?

What kind of candy do you like to give out?

Do you carve jack-o-lanterns?

NOV · *Election Day*

Do you vote on Election Day?

Are you a Democrat or a Republican?

How do you feel about the way we elect our leaders?

Who was the best (worst) politician you ever voted for?

Veterans Day   NOV

What branch of the military have you served in?

Have you seen action & where?

Were you ever wounded?

What medals have you earned?

What is the most interesting place in which you have been stationed?

NOV   *Ramadan*

What does the celebration of Ramadan mean to you?

How do you and your family observe this holiday?

What kind of meals do you have after your daily fast?

What do you know about the Five Pillars of Faith?

Have you ever made a pilgrimage to Mecca?

Thanksgiving Day　NOV

Where do you usually spend Thanksgiving Day
With whom do you most often spend it?
What do you like most about this holiday?
Who does all the cooking?
What is you favorite thing to eat?
What are you most thankful for in your life?

DEC   *Hanukkah*

What is the best present you ever got?
What was this holiday like for you when you were a child?
Who do you usually celebrate this holiday with?
Do you make or eat any special foods?

Winter Begins DEC

What do you like (hate) most about winter?
What was the biggest snowstorm you ever experienced?
Do you like or hate the cold?
Have you ever built a snowman?
Do you like to snow ski?
Do you vacation to a warm climate?

DEC

Kwanzaa

What does the celebration of Kwanzaa mean to you?
Who do you usually celebrate this holiday with?
Do you decorate your home in any special way for the holiday?
Do you prepare a special meal?
Do you know the seven principles of Kwanzaa?
Do you know the correct way to light the Kinara?
What words in African languages do you know?

Christmas   DEC

What kind of tree do you get and how do you like to decorate it?

How old were you when you stopped believing in Santa?

Who is the first one in your family to look under the tree Christmas morning?

Who do you usually spend this holiday with?

What was the best present you ever received?

140
Video Family History

Rob and Laura Huberman are the co-authors of *Video Family Portraits: The User Friendly Guide To Videotaping Your Family History, Stories and Memories* (Heritage Books, 1987).

Rob has produced and directed television programs for education, entertainment, public relations, news, and public affairs, and has received several awards for programming excellence. He earned his B.A. in Communication from The American University in Washington, D.C. and has taught television production courses in studio production, field production and editing at the elementary, high school and adult levels. Rob is the former managing editor of a weekly newspaper and is currently the publisher at ComteQ Communications in Margate, New Jersey.

Laura is a psychotherapist in private practice in Linwood, NJ and has conducted support groups and workshops for individuals and healthcare professionals. She was formerly with the Washington, D.C. Bureau of CNN, where she assisted in the production of the morning news and was also the producer for a cable television music entertainment program. Laura earned her B.A. in English from the University of California at Berkeley and received a Masters Degree in Social Work from the Catholic University of America in Washington, D.C.

Use this form, call customer service at 800-247-6553 or order online at www.comteqcom.com

ORDER ADDITIONAL COPIES BY CHECK, MONEY ORDER, OR CREDIT CARD

QTY	TITLE	1-4	5-10	11 & UP		TOTAL
	Video Family History	$14.95	$9.00	CALL	BOOK TOTAL	
					NJ RESIDENTS ADD 6% SALES TAX	
SHIPPING (USPS Priority -- call 609-487-9000 for other options) **$3.85** FIRST BOOK/ **$1.00** EACH ADDITIONAL BOOK					SHIPPING TOTAL	
You can also order online at www.comteqcom.com					TOTAL ENCLOSED	

SHIPPING INFORMATION

Name

Address

City   ST   Zip

(_____) _____

Dat time phone   Email

Special Instructions

BILLING INFORMATION

Name on credit card

Billing Address (if different from shipping

City   ST   Zip

credit card#

circle one   *VISA*   MasterCard   Exp. Date _____

Signature

Mail to: COMTEQ PUBLISHING • P.O. BOX 3046 • MARGATE, NJ 08402 • (609) 487-9000
Please allow 5-7 days for delivery

A fun & easy way to preserve and pass on your family history!

Makes a great birthday or holiday gift.

To order additional copies:
Use order form on previous page

Call 1-800-247-6553

Visit *Video Family History* on the web at www.comteqcom.com